Mindful Minutes

A Marketer's Journey Through Business

Sonya Ruff Jarvis

Author

Enhanced
DNA
DEVELOP. NURTURE. ACHIEVE.
Publishing Division

Enhanced DNAPublishing

•

Sonya Ruff Jarvis

.

13 I can do all this through him who gives me strength.

Philippians 4:13 NIV

Sonya Ruff Jarvis

Mindful Minutes

A Marketer's Journey Through Business

First Edition

ISBN-13: 978-1-7336477-1-7

Cover Created by Andrea Greene
Enhanced DNA: Develop Nurture Achieve Publishing
www.EnhancedDNAPublishing.com

Dedication

For my Mom, who taught me to be present in the moment and to make every minute count, because we do not know what tomorrow will bring.

Thank you Mom.
Rest in Peace.

Acknowledgments

I want to thank my husband, who has taken the time to read, review and comment on every word that I have written for publication, and my daughter, for the joy she brings into the many mindful minutes that we have shared. Thank you to my oldest brother and my sister for their daily support and love. A special word of appreciation to my publisher who encouraged me and helped turn the adaptation of Sonya's Blog into a book.

Foreword

By Deborah Shearer

Marketing is my passion. It excites me and it motivates me. It requires us to understand what the customer wants, how to deliver it to them and if you're a good marketer, even to be slightly crazy. If you have *Mindful Minutes: A Marketer's Journey Through Business* in hand, you're probably a marketer yourself, and as passionate about the subject as I am. And, if you truly believe in the quote "if you dream it, you can do it" by Walt Disney, you'll also believe in the woman behind this inspiring journey, MBA marketer, entrepreneur, SBO, wife and mom, Sonya Ruff Jarvis.

I have known Sonya for more than ten years. You could say we "grew up in the business together". Sonya called me one day to participate in a Channel Leader program she developed for the Hardware industry and to enlist me as a new product judge. Years later as Sonya launched her current business, the eRetailer Summit; she enlisted me on her Advisory Board. It was clear then as it is now that Sonya has exceptional leadership skills, a vibrant personality and is one of those "get it done" people you just need to know. Her style is very much like what you'll see through her book, work, blog and her personal life on the pages to follow; as she shares her expertise and introduces her family, including her husband and daughter.

I suggest you take this journey with Sonya and use this book as inspiration first, and then as a guide for instruction, striving for excellence, achieving it, sometimes falling short, learning from those experiences and ultimately, creating a successful business.

"Give light to your life's passion" – Sonya Ruff Jarvis

Congratulations, Sonya!

Sonya Ruff Jarvis

Table of Contents

Sonya Ruff Jarvis

*"Your work is going to fill a large part of your life,
and the only way to be truly satisfied is to do what
you believe is great work."*

Steve Jobs

Introduction

This book is based on Sonya's Blog: Breaking the Code of Excellence, a Jarvis Consultants LLC product. It was created to examine the mystery around striving for excellence, achieving it, and yes, often falling short. Evaluating the results we are faced with as business professionals and as consumers; what are the lessons learned through every day experiences? Sonya's Blog: Breaking the Code of Excellence shares up-close mindful minutes through personal encounters that are interesting, and quite frankly deserve more thinking and conversation.

Beginnings are always about starting something new, searching and defining who we are. Part I, Creating, will focus on the meaning of our contribution to life, business, community and ultimately our families. Are you consciously making decisions to contribute and what does that ultimately mean? Are you enjoying what you're doing? If not, is it worth the sacrifice? It just might be, but please be sure because life is short and we don't get replays.

Part II, Learning, focuses on all of those learnings and discoveries that we experience each and every day. What are you doing with them? It's easy to get caught up in our busy lives and not look at what is staring us in the face. I challenge myself to understand what is being put before me each day; and try to do something with it. It might mean putting a project on hold and, focusing on family. Whatever it is, approach it with your eyes wide open.

Who doesn't want to gain more marketing tips & tactics? As I journey through my life experiences, I always love to find good tips and tactics to share. Learning never stops and using real-life encounters makes it somehow seem more relevant and yes, even more applicable to our businesses and marketing plans. Tips are as good as your use of them, and tactics we know are all about the execution. Part III, Executing, will explore, analyze and share some successful business tips & tactics.

Part IV, Experiencing, pushes us to be present in our encounters each and every day. There are consequences to every action. It can be a good result or a bad result; and, in my book an indifferent result falls right under bad result. Are you measuring your interactions with brands and customer service associates to determine if that brand should get your time, attention and hard-earned cash? Being open minded but critical is important to making conscious decisions or whether you will participate in that

Brand's journey. This chapter will share experiences that will challenge us to be more aware in the future.

Sonya's Blog takes us through a marketer's journey of mindful minutes, extrapolating life experiences and turning them into business lessons learned.

Enjoy the read.

"If you can dream it, you can do it."

Walt Disney

Part I:

Creating...

Life is short.

That's not a cliché. It's a reality that gets clearer with each passing day (for me anyway).

When you think about life, what do you dream about? Ultimately, what do you want to do with your days? How are you contributing to the world, your legacy and your life?

Heavy questions? You bet! Questions that most of us, claim we are too busy to stop, think about and search for, the answers. And, before you know it, life has passed us by.

The following experiences are great examples of passions, causes, good ole' fun and dreams to consider as you strive to live your dream; and, find the passion that drives you forward. Hopefully, these encounters will challenge you to ask those heavy questions that, when answered, will lighten and illuminate your life's passion.

Do You Believe?

When my daughter was 10, she asked me if Santa Claus is real. Before I answered the question I was curious as to why she was asking. Well, a classmate (a year older) told her Santa didn't exist. My next question to her was, "Do you want the truth?" She assured me that she really wanted to know if Santa was real.

I explained that while there is not a man in a red suit steering a sleigh and distributing gifts across the world that the spirit of Christmas is REAL. It's a special time celebrated around the world that gives hope and happiness to many. The season also gives us reassurance that "believing" crosses all aspects of our lives including business.

But when it comes to our businesses, what are we believing in and how are we showing it? Is there an initiative that is done because it's the right thing to do but your margins aren't necessarily the company standard? Or, are you doing pro bono work offering your expertise to a group within your community that needs your services?

I have a dear friend who has inspired me to believe even when it's not Christmas! He has run successful businesses over his career; and he knows how to creatively put things together and get things done. He spearheaded an idea that would give back to the community in a big way. Jerid O'Connell led the charge to create the trail through the H. Smith Richardson Wildlife Preserve in Westport, CT identifying and organizing volunteers and local environmental nonprofits. The project was based on cleaning up, clearing out and getting scores of businesses to participate from the donation of new trees to organic juices.

As I was looking out over the field of new trees at the Wildlife Preserve, I thought, "this is my friend's, his family's and the community's legacy". The trail will be shared with so many generations and will exist long after each era is gone.

Believing in something bigger than ourselves drives us to be better and do better. It also challenges us to make a difference wherever we decide to invest our time and talent.

And, while my daughter didn't take the truth very well about Santa, she made the ultimate decision to still believe...I hope you still believe in something too...

Do You Shop Small?

Do you make an effort to shop small in your local community?

It's true that small businesses are the backbone of the US economy. Did you know that small businesses represent 99.7% of all US businesses? Not only do small businesses make up nearly half of non-farm GDP, they cumulatively employ roughly 48% of the US workforce. All these facts are reported by Small Business Profile in the US Small Business Administration Office of Advocacy.

American Express founded an annual movement back in 2010 that promotes the importance of supporting smaller businesses in communities across America. It's called Small Business Saturday and is now considered a holiday shopping tradition. Small Business Saturday takes place the Saturday after Thanksgiving.

Did you know that for every $100 dollars spent locally with independent businesses that $48 gets reinvested back into the local community? Meanwhile, the opposite is true when you spend that same $100 at chain stores. A mere $14 gets reinvested back into the community.

If we take all of the above mentioned data out of the

equation, independent businesses give back so much more to our communities. Besides the investment in the local economy, they also bring new ideas, innovation, and a commitment to invest in our communities. But more importantly, as Paul Nugent writes for ShopKeep, small businesses help create the community's identity, and they keep the tax dollars within the community, among a whole host of other reasons.

This is not only true on the consumer side; the *North America Retail Hardware Association* and *Independent We Stand* organizations, recently completed a study where it shows the same is true for the professional side of home improvement. Builders, contractors and trades people can impact their local communities by buying local.

The bottom line is that small businesses keep our local economy strong and that just feeds into the national economy. And, it's all personal because the small business customer represents your friends, relatives and neighbors. If you think about it, it's odd that we have to be nudged to shop small. Because small businesses often have the unique items and customized services, and who wouldn't want those?

I really do love independent businesses. You find a passion and energy that is contagious and makes you want to be part of something that is different and personal.

So after we come out of our food coma from Thanksgiving, let's think BIG and shop SMALL and join the Small Business Saturday movement.

Nice To Meet The Grommet

It's always an interesting journey to visit a retail company's headquarters and learn more about that company's mission, its people and its values. And, the best part, you learn all about the brand right in its headquarters directly from the employees living and breathing the mission and the values of the corporation. I took a drive up to Somerville, Massachusetts (an interesting side note the GPS address is Cambridge, MA) to visit and learn more about The Grommet at its headquarters.

A huge thanks to Ryan DeChance, Director, Discovery and Meredith Doherty, VP of Discovery, for their hospitality. They were the perfect hosts!

I have been following The Grommet for years and they recently were recognized and awarded the "Design Influencer of the Year Award" by HomeWorld Business magazine.

The Grommet is known for approaching retail differently by discovering new innovative products and bringing them to market quickly; all the while celebrating the maker.

When I arrived at their HQ I realized I probably did not know as much about them as I thought. They are located in a two story brick building off of a sleepy side street. When I walked in, the lobby hit me with a display of products. My host, Ryan DeChance, pointed out some of the notable products displayed in the lobby that I might know like Mrs. Meyers' Natural Clean Day Products, the Fitbit and the Pocket Monkey, just to name a few brands that The Grommet helped to make household brand names.

Image Credit: Jarvis Consultants, LLC

It's an open air working environment where offices with doors line the perimeter of the building, and a couple of dogs play around with each other. The humor and creativity show throughout the office space.

Whether it is the coaster displayed on the side tables in the lobby with the co-founders photography, or the large chalkboard in the kitchen area that has a different playful question every other week.

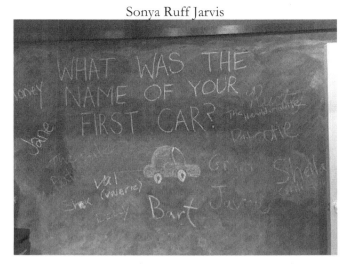

Image Credit: Jarvis Consultants, LLC

The personality of The Grommet was alive and well during my visit; displaying creativity, intelligence, fun, high-energy and hard-at-work employees. I want to share with you some information about The Grommet that I did not know.

- Their shoppers are 70% women.

- They really do launch at least one new product a day on their website. Sometimes two! Yes, you read correctly - each and every day!

- Once they identify an innovative product, they make sure that the maker has the expertise to succeed, and part of the process includes support with operations, PR, distribution, etc.

- They operate a wholesale arm in addition to direct to consumer.

- They operate a brick and mortar store and The Grommet features products in select Ace Hardware stores nationwide.

There is so much more that I discovered that cannot be covered here.

The one discovery that is the foundation of The Grommet values is that the co-founders found their passion and are living their dream.

What's Your "Cause"?

Alzheimer Walk, Norwalk, CT 2015
Image Credit: Alzheimer Association Connecticut Chapter
Calf Pasture Beach

Whether you are an independent business, big corporation or an individual, what's your "cause"? What are you fighting for to help your employees, customers, community, or even the world become a better place?

Does that sound cliché? Well it's not. Did you know that @engageforgood recently reported that Cause Sponsorship will reach $2.06 billion in 2017? By now, that number has probably exploded.

Many companies will support charitable initiatives that have been declared "the cause" for that particular month. Other companies will contribute to a lot of different charities while not committing wholly to any one cause, and that works for them. While others have a cause that reflects their mission statement and keeps them on track in representing their values both internally and externally by consistently contributing to a pre-determined charitable cause. Still, there is another group that evolves in the causes that they represent. It all depends upon the season that they are going through (in their business or in their lives) and whether the disease, natural disaster, etc. is affecting them or someone they know.

Whatever charitable cause you choose to connect your brand to, please make sure that it's genuine and that you truly believe in it. A recent Unilever study shows that 33% of consumers buy from brands doing social or environmental good. The major objective shouldn't be to drive traffic to your store, casino or website. Or, to increase sales because you're doing something charitable and want credit for it. If you are genuinely in it to make a difference, all of these benefits are by-products and will happen if you are committed for the long run.

Be fickle, uncommitted or fake and your efforts will be seen as that...

Be true, committed or real and your efforts will be seen as that...

The choice is yours.

I participated in the local Alzheimer's Walk to help raise money and awareness about this terrible disease in honor of my Mom. When my friend and I arrived at the walk area there was a huge Dunkin' Donuts tent with complimentary coffee, donuts and muffins. That jarred a pleasant memory for me that was more than a decade old. Yes, Dunkin' Donuts supported a breast cancer run that I had participated in for years in New York City's Central Park; and, I remember that I never knew that Dunkin' Donuts sponsored this event until the year I ran it as a breast cancer survivor. As a survivor, I had access to a VIP tent that offered complimentary Dunkin' Donuts treats.

Yes, a donut VIP tent was an awesome experience. Access to donuts, coffee, and special promotional items made me feel special, and I have to believe that subconsciously that was one of the reasons that I started making it a point to frequent Dunkin' Donuts.

So, whatever your "cause", know that, done right, it can have a lasting effect and build a loyal customer; all the while making the world a better place.

Tuesday Was An Interesting Day!

Tuesday May 22, 2018 was an interesting day for me, and, I am guessing for the retail home improvement b-to-b industry too. For me, I took the day off and went with my daughter on her school's 5th grade field trip to the Mystic Seaport, coined the Museum of America and the Sea in Mystic, CT.

For those of you who are not familiar with Mystic, CT, it is a small town in the southeastern part of the state that is along the Mystic River that flows into the Long Island Sound which is an access to the Atlantic Ocean. So, it is a seaside town and the Mystic Seaport Museum re-created the 19th century seagoing village NOT with replicas but real buildings fully staffed with the most amazing historians, storytellers, cooks and musicians. It is quite impressive and really brings history to life. It was a great field trip for the children, but all of the parents loved soaking in some history too!

We had an excellent tour guide who was a retired Librarian. She helped to refresh my memory; plus, I learned new things about 19th century living in Connecticut. The experience was enlightening and sometimes surprising, but definitely an interesting day for me.

Being involved in the home improvement business-to-business retail world, the internet was blowing up with breaking news while I was enjoying the field trip. We were asked (no, really told) to be role models to the students by not using our phones. So, I had no idea what was going on…until much later.

I finally read the news that a major CEO had left a retailer to head up the second largest home improvement mass retailer. Surprised? Yes, but it makes so much sense.

When DIY home improvement and hardware get under your nails it is hard to get it out. The hardware/home improvement industry has a way of pulling you in; and, while it is boring and un-exciting to many, there are also those of us who love the business. So, as I was walking around exploring and taking in the sites and literally watching history come alive before my own eyes, where was my gaze fixed?

You guessed it! What really caught my eye and interest were the old hardware and maritime stores.

Image Credit: Jarvis Consultants, LLC

This tiny village, back in the day, had its hardware store and its mass merchants that were central to the survival of villagers and seamen who relied on these products.

So, Tuesday May 22, 2018 was an interesting day because it reminded me that the hardware/home improvement industry means a lot to me, but it also means a lot to so many people out there that contribute to, and work in the industry.

From the outside, I understand why this executive went back to his hardware/home improvement roots, because it draws you in, and when you leave it, you miss it.

I bet he had an interesting Tuesday, too!

What Do You Do For Fun?

Image Credit: Jarvis Consultants, LLC

At the beginning of the summer I took a ride with my husband to the local Home Depot. He usually goes in, purchases what he needs and leaves. When I go with him he knows it'll be more of a discovery stroll. For fun and entertainment, I like to walk through the store (any store) and find out what they have new, hopefully get inspired through merchandising displays, and in this case, find any potential DIY project ideas that might be relevant to our home "to do" list. Well, we had been thinking about an outdoor gazebo area for a while, and the Home Depot had one displayed.

No, I really mean it. They had ONE displayed. There was no assortment of products, which is out of character for the Home Depot.

The displayed product didn't look that sturdy and we were disappointed that there weren't more to see. But, I realize gazebos are just one of those products that take up a lot of floor space. Essentially, it is prohibitive to line-up and display an assortment. When I actually looked closer at the displayed gazebo I saw that one of the columns of the structure had a wrap-around promotion sign. On that wrap they were promoting additional gazebos that are available at homedepot.com.

Good idea!

The sign had colorful photos with descriptions and specs, which brings me to the beauty of online shopping and the assortment of choices offered. Online is not limited to floor space or accommodating other merchandise in the area. There can actually be a limitless number of gazebos online for me and my husband to consider purchasing. The negative is that we can't touch it, feel it, stand in the middle of it - you get the picture. We can't physically experience the product.

By showcasing the Home Depot assortment of gazebos on a column wrap that you can find online, the consumer is offered the best of both worlds.

Since we experienced a display of the gazebo at the store, it

gave us a "feel" for the merchandise. So, physic
standing in the middle of one gave us a great sense of th
product details of the others. But the Home Depo
offered the opportunity to explore, virtually at our
convenience, their gazebo assortment online. The store
brought it to our attention that we have more than what
you are seeing.

It's a good idea because they are not relying on the
consumer to take the leap and think to look online; or,
waiting for a Home Depot associate to tell the customer
that there is more online.

I believe as we move forward in this ecommerce world that
cross merchandising in-store with online will be the
ultimate in capturing product sales and customer loyalty.
And, as more and more physical stores begin to offer an
online shopping experience we will see more of this in-
store marketing tactic. We see merchandising evolve as the
retail world continues to change.

By the way, in case you're wondering, we didn't purchase
the gazebo.

If You Can Dream It, You Can Do It!

I love that quote by Walt Disney, *"If You Can Dream It, You Can Do It"*, because every time I read it, I am inspired to believe in my dreams. I have actually used that piece of inspiration under my signature on my emails for the past several years, to remind me that dreams do come true. And, that very quote also started this section of the book.

And, one of my business dreams came true.

A dream that was founded on listening to the needs of customers and filling a void in the marketplace launched October 26, 2016 in Fort Lauderdale, FL. It's called the Home Improvement eRetailer Summit, an intimate gathering focused on education, building relationships, and understanding how to approach the Home Improvement eCommerce market.

Thanks to great partners, perseverance, progressive leaders in the eCommerce space, and great speakers, the first event hit the mark, and it is now an annual Summit.

So, I'm grateful that all of the parts came together; and, when times were challenging that my partners and I, unequivocally knew that when you listen to what customers want/need and you build it, they will come. What are your customers telling you?

Believe that, if you can dream it, you can do it.

I did!

"Learn from the mistakes of others. You can't live long enough to make them all yourself."

Eleanor Roosevelt

Part II

Learning…

We are all learners. From the time that we are born, we begin to learn everything – from taking our first breath, eating, crawling, walking, talking. Everything. Some things we learn without effort; some from trial and error. As we continue to mature and grow, we begin to challenge ourselves to learn more, do more and we often learn through our mistakes. Sometimes we watch, observe and even attempt to learn from others' and when we observe their mistakes, we do so to keep from making the same error.

In the business world, we often call learning from others

and implementing processes from those successes, "best practices". We are often eager to understand how someone else approached a challenge and found a solution. Perhaps, we will be able to apply it to our own business challenge in some way.

However, it is my belief that the lessons that truly stick with us come from our up-close and personal experiences. These experiences have guided some best practices in my business resulting in multiple successes.

In order to get to those best practices, you have to go through some learning, your own personal journey. The following pages represent some examples from my personal journey.

Happy New Year!

As we welcome in a New Year we all should take the time to reflect on those new acquaintances we met through the year, all of our life-long acquaintances and especially to remember those dear acquaintances who we lost.

If your life is anything like mine, the past year has brought both joy and sadness; triumphs and failures; victories and defeats. But, the beauty that is consistently evident in each situation is that I have never faced any situation alone. Whether it be family, friends, or business associates, someone has always had my back. Each acquaintance brings an opportunity to forge deep relationships that we cherish, and they are present to celebrate, to encourage or to cry with, depending on the circumstance.

So, as we say goodbye to one year and we usher in a new one, please let us appreciate each and every acquaintance we have met along the way. Most of us associate Robert Burns' poem, that he wrote in 1788, with ringing in the New Year. Here is a portion:

Auld Lang Syne

Should auld acquaintance be forgot,
and never brought to mind?
Should auld acquaintance be forgot,
and auld lang syne?

CHORUS:
For auld lang syne, my jo,
for auld lang syne,
we'll tak' a cup o' kindness yet,
for auld lang syne.

Cheers to each and every one of my acquaintances and the best for a happy, healthy and prosperous New Year!

When Was The Last Time You Checked Out?

Image Credit: Jarvis Consultants, LLC

Recently, I checked out. I literally checked out of my day-to-day life for a full week. I left my family and my business behind on a sad minute's notice to focus on one priority - my Mom.

You see hospice, called to inform us that my Mom probably had little time left on this earth, and she lived a plane ride away. My amazing husband and daughter supported my hectic effort to catch the next available plane to spend time with her.

The last week of her life I was with her. I was not thinking about anything else but my one priority, my Mom. Focused on being present, breathing the same air, sharing the same space, making sure she was comfortable and well taken care of. But most importantly, talking to her and letting her know what a wonderful Mom, friend, and counselor she had been to me my entire life.

I have never checked out before where I had one sole focus. I was thankful I had the support that I could do it. Being present for my Mom's last breath was a blessing to me and, I pray, for her, too.

Now, I'm trying to be more present in all that I do. Whether it's listening to my daughter's complex school stories or watching a game winning play of my husband's favorite team that he DVR'd for me; or, being empathetic about a customer's challenge and figuring out how to be part of the solution.

There are times in our lives where we must pause.

This was a time where I stopped. I stopped everything including Sonya's blog.

I want to let you know that I had a good reason. And, that the blog will resume being published every other Thursday starting today.

I have officially checked back in.

How Hard Is It For You To Just Say No?

It's always interesting to me that people find it hard to say "no". I am talking about the people that don't say yes either. Right, you know what I'm talking about. If you have been in business for any length of time you have come across people who just can't say no but they don't say yes.

Many believe that when you never respond that it should be accepted as the universal "no".

Yet, just saying no from the beginning would save so much time and money. I believe saying no should be considered a standard of excellence in conducting oneself with professional etiquette. I would guess that most people would appreciate that response and see it as a respectful gesture that you don't want to waste anyone's time including your own.

- Say no if you're not interested.
- Say no if you're don't want the person on the other end to call you back.
- Say no if you don't want emails and voice mails clogging your inbox.

But for some reason, the majority of us just can't say "no".

I did some research on this topic only to find out that while this phenomenon has been talked about and written about at exhaustive levels it is mostly about people who always say "yes". An article written by Hank Davis from *Psychology Today* put it best "*...they are far more comfortable having your request die of old age than actually refusing it. They'll leave it for you to figure out whatever it was you wanted just ain't gonna happen*".

Really? Just say "no thank you".

Here are my top 5 reasons why we just can't say "no". They are:

1. The Universal language of "no": By not responding you get the message. *(We already talked about this, which I believe is the #1 reason.)*
2. Avoiding Tension/Conflict: Uncomfortable saying no because we don't want tension or conflict.
3. Hedging our Bets: Thinking about the issue because we don't want to entirely close the door. It's just like the lottery – "You never know".
4. Too Busy: Believing that we are too busy to stop and take the time to respond.
5. Not Relevant: It's just not relevant to our business/being. (This is the most justifiable reason but still just respond "no".

That makes a lot of sense intellectually; and, admittedly, I'm not a psychologist (even though I did consider Psychology as a Minor as an undergraduate, for a moment). But it's my guess that it's more of an emotionally-driven non-response. Either way, like the lyrics of a popular song by the group, A

Great Big World, states, *"Say something, I'm giving up on you"*. But, wouldn't it be so much easier to just say "no"?

> *"Focusing is about saying no"*
> *Steve Jobs*

The Buck Stops Here!

A good leader always wants to empower team members to honestly voice their ideas, suggestions and opinions. It takes a host of different departments to implement any successful business initiative. Each area needs to be proficient in its core competency (i.e. finance, merchandising, human resources, marketing, etc). There are so many cross-functional activities that need to be performed well by different departments to yield the best results.

It happens in both small and big business especially when the company is stretching out of its comfort zone to reach for aggressive goals or a new vision. Inevitably, the lines of responsibilities can get blurred. I believe that this happens through sheer interest and the desire to contribute, but team members begin influencing decisions that are outside of their core competency. Honestly, it's fun to be engaged and know that our opinion counts. But we always need to pause and check ourselves because it's important that team members express their opinions based on their expertise. It becomes dangerous when the advice is not grounded in our discipline or knowledge of our customer base. The scales then begin to become unbalanced, and now there are influencers weighing in that just might tip it to make the final decision.

When this type of decision-making starts to happen, accountability begins to erode and a group consensus emerges. It's always good to have group buy-in because it makes the execution process that much smoother. But, ultimately there always needs to be a singular person (the leader) who is responsible for the final decision. Otherwise, there is no accountability.

And, we all know that accountability is important in each and every business. Not for the "gotcha" moment but the business that runs best is based on established objectives, goals and measurements and will fundamentally always achieve higher results.

Good leaders navigate through challenges by recognizing the situation, knowing that the buck stops with them, and stepping up to own the accountability.

What's Your Excuse?

Image Credit: Jarvis Consultants, LLC

We headed down to Hilton Head, South Carolina for the last vacation before school started, but when we booked our trip we didn't realize that South Carolina was the only state that the Eclipse would appear in its totality. So, when we arrived at the airport and proceeded to our rental car counter we had no idea what was in store for us. As a Preferred Avis loyalty member we are accustomed to whizzing into our car and driving out of the airport. Nice and easy, right? Well not this time.

First, this particular Avis location does not have Preferred Service where you proceed directly to your car; but there is a designated line where they have your car rental agreement and keys waiting and ready to go. Well, our agreement was there, but no keys. As the representative was waiting on me, it became clear that there was a shortage of cars. She assured me there was a car for my family, but because of the Eclipse they were sold out and having a hard time turning the cars around as needed. She asked us to wait and she'd let us know when to go and get our keys and car. There was a gentleman that was waited on behind us and, he too, was waiting for the "high" sign that would indicate that our cars were ready. I asked if he had Preferred Service and he said "yes". He also voluntarily shared that he never experienced this before. Meanwhile, the customer service person overheard us talking and explained once again that they couldn't help it. It wasn't their fault, it was because of "the Eclipse."

The last Eclipse like this was 99 years ago. They knew this one was coming due to the amount of publicity. It didn't take the world by surprise. When once in a lifetime world events happen in your business path you best get prepared. To think you can handle the situation like Christmas or Thanksgiving minimizes the largeness of the event. You not only want to optimize revenues but maintain your customer service levels and protect the integrity of your brand. Customers are rarely forgiving even if they are loyal. Customers just want what they want when they want it; and, figure since they paid for it they should get it - no excuses.

So, while you might not have made excuses about the

Eclipse, think back about the last excuse you made to a customer about why your business didn't deliver.

Customers don't care about excuses, so here are some tips for Avis or any business facing an external activity that has the potential to compromise your customer service:

- Get ready and adjust processes for that day;
- Alert customers who might be affected when they book the reservation;
- Remind customers the day before that there might be delays due to the volume of Eclipse watchers;
- If you're face to face, thank the customer for their loyalty and reiterate what is happening, but don't use it as an excuse;
- Send them a follow up thanking them and apologizing if the customers experienced a delay.

So, the next time you're explaining to a customer why they aren't getting "whatever", stop, change the conversation to why you value them, why their loyalty is important to you and your business, and why you will continue to work hard to earn their business.

By the way, viewing the Eclipse (and our vacation) was an amazing and memorable experience, very much worth the wait!

Don't Forget About The Old While Chasing The New

Like many, I'm a big believer in attracting new customers that are the right profile for the brand. However, I have never believed that you invest the majority of your resources into attracting new customers. It's important to always have a two prong approach where you invest in not only maintaining but also, delighting your existing customers. In many ways, it's much easier and affordable to work hard to keep an existing customer.

Did you know that it cost 5 times more to attract a new customer than to retain an existing customer? That is a good reason to invest marketing dollars and focus on growing a relationship with existing customers. It even costs less! Even though they are cheaper to maintain, loyal customers are priceless!

Regardless of the data that consistently backs up investing in current customers, there are instances where brands chase after those one-time wonders; making the deal so sweet that a "new" prospective customer can't pass it up. So, they try it, and when the deal is no longer available, they drop the brand.

Why?

Because the relationship started out wrong. Like any good relationship you have to be in it for the long run and invest the time. Establishing a loyal customer has to start out as a reciprocal relationship (i.e. the customer is getting something from the brand and the brand is gaining something - the customer).

The brand has to pique the interest of the prospective customer and entice his/her curiosity enough for the first transaction to take place. Once the customer tries the brand now the brand has to show that it will consistently deliver what the customer expects.

That's when the romance starts.

The brand has to literally make the customer feel a visceral emotion whether he/she is happy, safe, beautiful - you get the point. Once that happens, boom! The brand has a loyal customer!

But this loyal customer can't and/or shouldn't be taken for granted. The brand has to keep the interest of the customer and keep making the customer feel that same intense emotion each and every time which, even for the biggest and best brands, is a challenge.

If the brand successfully develops a strong relationship, shows the customer that they value him/her, keeps delighting and romancing the customer to feel that desired emotion, then the brand will have a loyal customer. So, pay close attention to your existing customers. Value them. But most importantly, don't forget about the old while you're chasing the new. Keep investing and focusing on your existing customers. It will always pay off.

Five Reasons Why Big Isn't Always Better

Image Credit: Jarvis Consultants, LLC

My nephew is a senior in high school (that's him #44) and happens to be a darn good football player. He has a number of colleges scouting his talent to play at their school. While it might appear to him that the Division I schools are the best because of their sheer size and their investments in their sports program, he was encouraged by his parents to look at smaller Division III schools because they might better fit his needs.

Why do we always think bigger is best? In some cases that is true, but not in all instances; and, we need to evaluate each situation on its own merit taking into account our needs and goals.

Recently I pitched a speaking role to a company. Based on all conversations, they liked what was being presented — the topic, the target, the end goal EXCEPT the audience wasn't big enough. They like to go BIG.

Believe me, I get that but not when all the other marks have been hit. So, whether it is a decision to attend a school, speak at an event or to accept a position at a company, consider that the biggest choice isn't always the best decision.

Here are my 5 reasons why big isn't always best.

1. Quality versus Quantity: Small counts as quality. Quality is intentional, takes effort and has a distinct intelligent purpose; Quantity is all about numbers.

   "Quality is more important than quantity. One home run is much better than two doubles."
   Steve Jobs

2. Focus versus Distractions: Focus counts as attention. Focus is directing time and attention to a smaller number of issues. Distractions are all about disruption.

   "My success, part of it certainly, is that I have focused in on a few things." Bill Gates

3. Unique versus Individual: Unique counts as not comparable. Unique is unparalleled, unmatched and unequal. Individual is all about making up a group.

> *"Each of us is a unique strand in the intricate web of life and here to make a contribution."*
> *Deepak Chopra*

4. Meaningful versus Shallow: Meaningful counts as significant. Meaningful is genuine, relevant and important. Shallow is superficial.

> *"A meaningful silence is always better than a meaningless word."*
> *Anonymous*

5. Follow-up versus Fall-thru: Follow-up counts as results-oriented. Follow-up is the ability to do what you said you were going to do. Fall-thru is nothing.

> *"To build a long-term, successful enterprise, when you don't close a sale, open a relationship." —*
> *Patricia Fripp*

Being in an environment with a small group considered a quality target gives us the opportunity to focus on the issue at hand. It gives us the chance to learn about the uniqueness of that person. It allows us to have meaningful conversations in a way that instills passion. When all of these forces come together follow-up is easy because we know exactly who we are talking to and the points to be made.

So, when considering whether to join, attend or accept please look at other parameters in addition to size. Because….. big isn't automatically always the best.

Ten Lessons From 2018

As a small business owner operating in an industry surrounded by large companies, I have learned so many lessons as I boldly dare to compete. Here are my top 10 business lessons learned in 2018.

1. Quantify everything!

    - If it can't be quantifiable it better darn sure be anecdotal!
    - If it's neither quantifiable nor anecdotal - dump it!

2. Don't expect reciprocity - it rarely happens!

    - If companies or people do not deliver the first time they will not deliver the second time. Stop expecting it and let them go.

3. People say all kinds of things because they don't know what to say...listen, correct what you can then move on!

4. Be willing to have tough conversations filled with honesty and frankness while being sensitive.

5. Always have multiple plans.

6. Results supersede everything (no excuses, no explanations). The bottom line is, do not believe the hype, especially when it is not backed up with numbers.

7. Stretch by trying different things and communicate with people you don't know.

8. Always be willing to learn something new. Never ever walk away without something new from a conference, article, or conversation.

9. Keep at it! Do not get discouraged, or if we do, let that feed our will to continue. In most cases, it does work out!

10. Take time to have fun, relax and restore our energy. We can't power through if we are running on a deficit.

There were many more lessons learned, but the above are truly my top 10. I felt that they needed to be written down as a quick reference to remind me of the things I should be doing as I boldly move into a new year.

"Opportunity is missed by most people because it is dressed in overalls and looks like work."

Thomas Edison

Part III

Executing...

Nothing of any value, comes easy. Some big accomplishment can appear that it was simple, from the surface, but behind that appearance of simplicity, there was lot of strategy, planning and execution. The strategy, planning and execution was critical for the result to be excellent. For marketers, 80% of the projects we work on never get to fruition; so, the 20% better really hit the mark (whatever it may be)!

Realize though, that strategy and planning can go very well, but if the execution goes awry, then the entire campaign can fail. Execution is key and that's where the real work comes in! I'm sure that you have heard the phrase, "the devil is in the detail". That phrase is spot on, because you have to think of every possible detail from the strategy or it could take a nasty turn. It's important to consider all options in your plan and play it out.

So, here are some good, bad and ugly (not really) experiences of executing business objectives or goals.

What Have You Done Lately?

Image Credit: Jarvis Consultants, LLC

What have you done lately to market your brand, products and services in a big way? I mean really big? I have witnessed two really good examples in the last month that made me think and I'd like to share them with you.

Here's the first encounter. I was recently walking through the Charlotte Douglass airport in North Carolina and saw this big, bold, beautiful promotion board. It was attractive and simple but what really drew my eye was the largeness of the board. Plus, the promotion drawings matched the physical size of the board. We (operative word here because I mean me too) have a tendency to promote our products and services consistently but do we go big and bold? Are our services big in the face of our prospects? Or do they have to look to find our services? Are we bold in showing our current clients what we have accomplished to move their business forward? Or do we feel like that's what we are being paid for; so why highlight the success?

Here are some great tips to help us stretch ourselves to be big and bold that are best practices that I learned from this experience.

Images say a thousand words; finding and using the right photography is important in making a bold statement. In this case, drawing the image. Look closely at the board where there are drawings of menu items.

Copy, in most instances, accomplishes more with less words. But the words we use should be strong to depict our messaging.

The second experience, I was watching a reality TV Show (yes I confess to watching reality TV) called Million Dollar Listing New York.

A real estate agent was trying to convince his client (a developer) to accept an offer. The developer had given him 100 houses to sell within a short period for the asking price; no exceptions! Which by the way, the agent had exceeded the milestone goals. There was one house not worthy of the developer's asking price but a buyer had put in a "decent" offer. The client was unwilling to accept the offer and threatened the agent to pull the rest of the business from him.

Well, the real estate agent had to remind his client exactly what he accomplished in a short period. He showed his client a huge box of signed contracts at the asking price representing more than half of the houses the developer gave him to sell.

The agent went bold and big in showing through actual materials his amazing results for the client. We need to track and know our accomplishments. And, then share them with our clients. So, don't be shy. We all need to go big and bold in promoting our brands, products and services.

Even Wonder Woman Needed Steve And Crew

Have you seen the Wonder Woman movie, Rise of the Warrior? My daughter saw it while I was away. I can still hear the excitement in her voice about the movie when I called home that night to check-in. She said that the Wonder Woman movie "inspired" her. I asked, "how"? She went on to tell me about the movie and how Wonder Woman was brave, courageous and fought for what she believed. So, I told my daughter I would like to see it, too, and she eagerly agreed that she would go with me.

Later that week, when we saw Wonder Woman together, I was proud of my daughter because for an almost 10 year old she summed it up pretty well. Wonder Woman was brave, courageous and willful. Arguably she possessed all of the characteristics of a leader. A leader who cares for her team, its mission and the greater good. Every true leader, in my opinion, also realizes that they are contributing to something that is greater than oneself, and clearly Wonder Woman recognized that purpose.

In the movie, Wonder Woman happened to team up with a character named Steve, who was a spy. The important thing that she learned from Steve was that she couldn't go it alone. Steve and Wonder Woman became partners in the mission, each needing one another. Steve also knew that to be successful they needed to form a complete team. Each team member he selected possessed the skills needed to help them accomplish the final objective. So, while Wonder Woman sometimes led with blind courage, her focus was always on accomplishing the goal.

Believe it or not, there are some valuable take away lessons from Wonder Woman's leadership skills that can be applied today, specifically for team members. They:

- need to understand each other's weaknesses and be empathetic, supporting one another;
- should have each other's back regardless of the circumstances because they recognize the greater good they are trying to achieve;
- need to respect decisions made as sacrifices to achieve the results;
- need to band together and be grateful regardless of the outcome.

Ultimate success and failures lay at our feet as leaders. But as we know, teams are important in accomplishing objectives and achieving results. And, no one person can do everything, all the time, consistently and excel. So, when you think you can go it alone, remember that Wonder Woman even needed Steve and crew to end World War I.

Pay It Forward

Have you ever heard the saying "do as I say and not as I do"? That always seemed ridiculous to me because why would I listen to someone whose words weren't reflected in their behavior? All credibility is lost when words don't reflect actions; because, even they can't do what they are saying to do...

Sounds simple, doesn't it?

That is, until it comes to us as Marketers.

I know for one, I want everyone who attends my events to complete a survey because I want to know about their experience so I can correct any issues for the future. Every time I call a customer or prospective customer about a new product or service, I want them to be just as excited as I am. I want them to spend significant time on the phone listening to why it's good for their company. And, what about those dreaded "pop up" windows asking for our opinions? How many times have you clicked on those to give your feedback? (I'm betting zilch!).

Why is it that we want everyone to take our surveys, give us feedback, listen to us, and return our phone calls? Especially, when we as Marketers aren't reciprocating or paying it forward when we are approached with the same.

Now here's my saying... "*If you believe in what you do then at least respect it when someone else does it*". Make sense? Bottom line, get engaged with the same type of marketing activities that we are asking others to participate in.

I can actually say that I do this, I participate and get involved. I answer telemarketing surveys, airline and hotel email surveys after the flight/stay and I even go in and log onto social media sites to post positive and negative experiences. Why? Because I know that those Marketers of those brands want to know. Believe me, my husband doesn't understand why I "waste" the time. I consider it an investment, particularly if I like the brand.

So, if you're a Marketer, "do as you expect", participate and engage by giving your feedback. Pay it forward because there is always the potential for it to come back tenfold.

March Madness

Who made a difference in your life besides your parents? As a mother of an elementary school child it is so evident the effect that teachers, coaches, and instructors have on our children's lives on a daily basis. I had a recent experience that I would like to share. It's especially relevant because it is the season for the Final Four NCAA Basketball Championships. We just finished up our version of the "final four" at our house.

My 9 year old daughter started her basketball season in October and it just ended late March – a long season – but typical these days. This was a new team for her; so, new team members, coaches, and plays. You get the picture. But it was also a step-up in level of play, complication of plays and expectancy of each team member's contribution. She was now in the big leagues (sort of), and it can be intimidating. She started out slow and then started getting her bounce, primarily because a coach saw her potential and started working specifically with her. His philosophy "execute successfully one play at a time". From that point forward, my daughter's confidence started building one play at a time.

This is a lesson that we need to be reminded of each and every day in our business lives. Who are we helping? Are we encouraging and recognizing potential in our colleagues, partners and employees? Are we approaching the opportunity to help someone in a planned, deliberate way? Here are some quick tips to help challenge ourselves to contribute to others growth and opportunity.

- Leave your biases behind – really look at each team player individually and then within context, based on evaluating the most potential in a skill set level that is currently needed.

- Evaluate what is lacking and what is needed to help that team member turn a weakness into a strength that can contribute to the overall team.

- Challenge ourselves to do what is good for the team member above all. While it's good for the company, the person should take priority. The people first rule always has good long-term karma.

- Be willing to correct and call the person out when they do something wrong, but also offer solutions to correct the error/problem.

So, make a decision to deliberately make a difference in someone's life by taking interest, actively managing, teaching and mentoring.

My daughter's team finished with 2 championships and a quarter final finish among 20 teams. The season's results were not a mishap – the coaches led the girls to a strong

March Madness finish executing successfully one play at a time. Enjoy the final four championships coming up!

Yippee! It's Over!

Yippee!!

Regardless of which side of the political party you represent, like me, I'm sure that you are glad that the 2016 presidential election year is over! It has caused much stress and anxiety and you can insert your own emotion(s) that you have been feeling in here to be included. I have talked to people across the country and regardless of party affiliation, many people had the same feeling – we couldn't wait until it was over.

Well, now it's over.

I'm sure that every discipline will be studying the 2016 presidential election for years to come. And, in my opinion, there were best practices that were evident that can be used by any marketer.

It's interesting to compare the elections to what many of us as marketers try to achieve each and every day in selling our brands, products and services. Promotions help to execute the strategy. But, telling our stories is what evokes that raw emotion and gives us the opportunity to make that connection with our consumers/customers/buyers.

Take the elections; two different stories were told. And, the arguments on both sides seemed pretty thematic.

It's my opinion that one campaign identified the target (after testing with focus groups, etc.) and started telling a story that they thought would resonate. They took the traditional approach. Another campaign, started talking, and talking, and a target audience emerged. This segment that emerged helped this campaign uncover the target audience and the messaging.

So, one campaign organically grew a self-identifiable group to target; a segment that had some common characteristics but spanned across a big portion of our country. It wasn't based on a formula, an approach, but rather a representation of the emerging group and then profiling (in this case) one's constituents, then identifying more like-constituents and taking their main concerns and crafting a story. It wasn't based on a pre-defined plan or strategy, but rather a marketing instinct to tap into a visceral emotion that became evident, stroked and appreciated by this group.

So, here's my question: When was the last time you looked at new emerging target customers and really listened to what they were telling you, then took their main concerns and crafted their story to sell your brand, products and services?

Remember even when our customers tell us something that might be difficult to hear, listen and put it to use by making your brand, products and/or services better.

So, put this lesson to work, and celebrate that the 2016 presidential election is over!

What Happened?

What happened?

I pre-ordered the new Hillary Rodham Clinton book, *What Happened*, and was looking forward to the delivery. And, as I was reading the book, I felt as though her assessment of what happened could be applied as an evaluation process for any business or project that has failed. How many times have we been profoundly disappointed in the outcome of a project? I know I have had major failures over the course of my career. While we can point to important accomplishments, those that were not achieved, haunt us. We didn't reach our goals and didn't deliver on the promise to our business, the company, and our employees. We all can fill in the blank. You get the picture.

We couldn't make it happen. End of story. Or is it really the beginning of the story?

How many of us take a step back and truly attempt to do a deep dive into why we were unsuccessful? I know for me, I always think I have it figured out along the way when things are going right. There are always one to two reasons why the initiative failed or the project didn't get off the ground. But, truth be told, it's hard to really do an honest post-mortem. Now I have my excuses for not engaging fully in that process, too. And, it all centers on time since there is never enough in one day. But if I (and I suspect all of us) want to be honest, it's hard to do a thorough self-evaluation. It's a difficult process to confront our own disappointments. But we have to force ourselves because it allows us to exercise an opportunity to clear that ghost out of the closet. That's the only way it won't haunt us. It also helps us to stop making the same mistakes and avoid pitfalls that are indicative of how we approach situations.

So, I believe anyone in business can identify with the words, "emotions" and "self-evaluation" in the book, *What Happened*. No one hits the mark 100% of the time.

As I continue to read this book, it has inspired me to dig deep and ask tough self-evaluation questions of my projects and my business. To really put myself out there and examine what I did or didn't do to contribute to missing the mark. It's hard to do but at one point or another I believe we can all challenge ourselves to ask, "what happened"?

It's The Most Magical Time Of The Year

Everywhere we go and everything we hear during the holiday season is an effort by world marketers to get us in the right frame of mind to spend money. The "magic of the season" creates a mood for us to loosen our wallets. In most cases, it starts right around, or after Halloween for many retailers. The more decorations, bright lights, Santa Claus', Christmas classics, and music that we see and hear nudges us that much closer to the holiday spirit. It reminds us that this is the time to focus on giving, not receiving. To remember all of the people that touch our lives like the mail carrier, the teachers, the distant cousin that we only see once a year; and, we buy gift cards, presents and experiences that will help to make those around us feel peace, joy and happiness.

As a marketer, the holiday season is the most optimal time of the year where we all start that infamous customer journey. While it touches all of us during the same time, we each will have different experiences and outcomes. And, the seller that taps into the mood the best, at the right moment, with the right offer, will win our hearts and cash for the season.

I don't know about you but my list is usually divided up where I can buy multiple folks the same gift; it's so much easier to buy, give and send the same gift to multiple people. I realized that I'm not the only one that thinks that way. A lady behind me today at a national chain store had 6 candles all in different colors; my sister's friend bought 72 of the same item to give to her team; and, my friend ordered books for her nephews and nieces all from the same store. Let's face it, as consumers we want a unique experience combined with easy solutions. We want to capture the magic of the season as quickly and for as long as we can; so if a retailer offers us solutions, we're there for the taking and happy to participate. But, only when we're absolutely ready to make that purchase decision.

So, we need to know our customers, talk with them on their terms, ask them what they want, help them with solutions for their holiday lists and above all make it easy for them. Because, our ultimate job as marketers during this season is to help make it the most magical time of the year where all of our customers can feel peace, joy and happiness.

Sonya Ruff Jarvis

Happy Sweetest Day!

I grew up in Ohio celebrating "Sweetest Day" every third Saturday in October. In my opinion, it is sort of like Valentine's Day for Ohioans (even though Hallmark says it is celebrated in all of the Great Lakes region). It was founded by Herbert Birch Kingston, a philanthropist, in 1922. It's not a state holiday but rather a national holiday. For some reason, few folks know about it that live outside of Ohio. I'm not sure why that is, other than Mr. Kingston lived and worked in Cleveland, Ohio; so, maybe having a native connection made a difference in its popularity.

The Founder began this holiday by giving candy to those in our society who were "forgotten". (Did I mention that he worked at a candy company?). His intentions were admirable. It was to bring happiness to those who are deprived, which at the time of the holiday's creation, was defined as orphans, shut-ins and the underprivileged.

Well, somewhere along the line the intention got muddled and it became a second Valentine's Day for Ohioans. We had school dances, gift giving and romantic expectations centered all-around Sweetest Day. Not once, did I ever think the "sweetest" was for someone other than a sweetheart. Sweetest Day was a big deal in my community growing up, but quite frankly it never caught traction in other parts of the country.

I didn't realize until college that everyone didn't celebrate Sweetest Day. When I would bring up the national holiday, I would be met with "what's that?".

So, as Sweetest Day approaches, I'm wondering why do some holidays make the annual published calendars and others don't? And, it's not that they just don't make the cut, these holidays are seen as obscure.

Like anything created to fulfill a need, there are expectations that it should evolve and be sustainable for the long term; unless we're talking about fads. So, founding holidays are much like creating a service or developing a new product. Here are some questions that we should ask ourselves when creating "new".

- Does it fill a national or global need, or is it contained to your local area?

- Can it survive on its own merit/benefits, or is it a "me too" brand because it's not that different from its competition?

- Does this (fill in the blank) fulfill a short or long-term need?

- How do you gain awareness and interest to create a long lasting brand?

These are not yes or no questions to answer; rather, they are questions to challenge us to think. Where are we going (the objective) and how long will it take us to get there (milestones); and, what is the endgame (goal)? It doesn't matter whether it's a new holiday, product, event, or service, it is essential that it delivers on a missing "need".

While, Sweetest Day isn't celebrated where I live now, every year on the third Saturday in October, I smile and remember all of my celebrated Sweetest Days of the past.

What's Your Follow-Up Like?

 A reminder to myself to follow up, be persistent but don't be a pest!

Regardless of the type of business we're in, research shows that the most successful people are those that consistently follow up. We can't get the sale if we don't follow up. We can't build a relationship if we don't follow up. To be able to follow-up successfully is clearly a skill and a characteristic that screams that you are different. Whether you are an attentive waitress or advertising executive, it is all about the follow up. Let's face it, most people just don't consistently follow up.

What's your follow up like?

When I truthfully answer this question, I know I have some work to do here. It's not because I don't follow up, but because I am one of "those people" that will continually follow up. For an example, if there is a "did not respond", I am going to try and connect with you in various ways until I hear the word "no". Some people appreciate the persistence and I think it makes them that much more interested in finally connecting. But, in most cases, I have to admit that the level of tenacity I bring to follow-up isn't always balanced; and, sometimes the scale can tip and prospects might (probably) think I'm a pest.

Every time I start thinking I'm a pest, I read research like this one from Dartnell Corp about following up on sales prospects. It's obvious that most people eventually give up but these numbers are staggering. Here they are:

- 48 % give up on the first contact;
- 73 % give up on the second contact;
- 84 % give up on the third contact;
- 90% give up on the fourth contact.

The premise of the study was based on the fact that persistence pays off; which, of course, makes perfect sense - that is, intellectually it makes sense. But, when you are facing rejection after rejection it becomes an emotional response to give up.

What statistical group do you fall-in?

If it's a lower one, don't feel bad. You can make it a point to develop stronger follow-up skills now. If you're in the higher group, congratulations! You're one of the 10% of salespeople that generate 80% of sales. It takes a disciplined person to follow up while continually hearing no. You see the end game and know the process is long. It's very clear, in most cases, the longer we continue to have meaningful follow-up with a prospect the greater opportunity to win a client. (The client sees that you care and that you're not going anywhere). It can be daunting but in the end the result is worth celebrating. If it were easy everyone would do it, right?

But it's not. It is well documented that it takes between 11-14 touches before someone buys. And, I can vouch for that in my business, too. Some might say that sounds high. But to me, it sounds right on point because you're including multiple layers of touches, including e-mail, social media, phone, and/or face to face meetings.

It's hard to make that many connections and to not be a pest. There will be definite times when the client might not appreciate the bugging. It's hard to do but we need to back off. (Or at least I do). But, I'm willing to admit that my follow-up needs more balance, and I plan to work on it.

What about you?

Sonya Ruff Jarvis

Your customer doesn't care how much you know until they know how much you care.

Damon Richards

Part IV

Experiencing…

The customers' journey is one that all brand owners want to understand and travel through in order to discover what the customer is truly feeling. Sometimes it is hard to grasp, because there are gaps between what many of us promise and what is consistently delivered. It is hard to evaluate, gauge and consistently promise. The elusive customer experience in delivering "delight" each and every time is a challenge, but we still chase it.

As you travel through each experience, undoubtedly you will recall some of your own customer encounters that were great, good or that you may want to forget.

Spying On Your Brand Promise

It has always bothered me that companies feel as though the boss needs to go undercover to discover if their employees are delivering on the brand promise. This approach seems like the "boss" is operating from a point of distrust and he/she is already signaling to the employees that there is a gap in what should be happening versus what is actually happening within the operations.

On the flip side, it bothers me that employees generally feel inhibited and helpless that they can't be honest with the company and share where cracks are beginning in the brand image and ideas that might make the brand that much better.

Fast forward to reality.

I believe that there is a much simpler way to determine if your employees are doing what they should be doing. First off, do the hard homework by getting to know your employees. Yes, have conversations (as in plural) with your folks who are on the front lines representing your brand name.

It is important that your employees understand what exactly you expect of them. There should be no assumptions or guessing games, rather:

- Established guidelines and policies; so employees understand the value and culture of your company and the standard for acceptable behavior;

- Make sure there are ongoing training programs that are consistent to ensure your employees are operating at your defined level of excellence;

- Set up performance evaluations that are equitable and help employees understand how their contributions are evaluated; and, more importantly, how they can succeed.

And yes, if you spot high-performing employees who have potential, invest in them so they feel valued; get them engaged and together map out a career plan.

Both you and your employee need to invest in a reciprocal relationship. By getting to know your employees, what uniquely motivates them and their life achievements/goals, it will enable you to help your employees deliver the best possible experience to your customers.

Operate from a point of trust and support. When you see a gap or a crack happening in delivering on your brand promise; intervene, evaluate, and help that employee. Sometimes you can't, and I trust that you'll know when that relationship needs to be terminated. But for the most part, you're dealing with people who want to contribute and give you their best.
So, when you're wondering what's really going on or your gut is telling you there is something wrong here, resist the

urge to find out by going undercover and face the issue openly and honestly. You'll be surprised what you'll discover.

When Did "Can I Help You?" Become A Rhetorical Question?

I stopped asking this question for a while, and now I answer it more from the sense of hope rather than thinking that I'm actually going to receive help. But it never fails, when I am in a store and I ask if they have my size, color, etc. Before I can get it out of my mouth the sales associate usually replies that everything we have is out on the floor. Really? Please enlighten me and just take a look (or at least pretend that you are looking). I realize that there are some cases where this is true and everything is indeed out on the floor. But, it can't possibly be true in every single case.

I had a recent experience where I decided to put that premise to the test. I stopped into a national chain store looking for the exact pair of jeans I had bought the previous month (and fallen in love with) from the same retailer but in a different town. I looked and couldn't find my size. I asked a sales associate for my size and surprise, I was told everything is out on the floor. I really wanted the jeans, so I pursued my mission and asked two other sales associates at two different times. Both gave me the same answer. I didn't notice but a fourth sales associate must have seen what was happening, and quietly went in the back and found the jeans in my size. She handed them to me. As I was walking out of the store with my purchase, I passed her and she looked at me and "mouthed" "sorry about that".

I can only assume she saw how my customer journey was playing out, and she decided to intervene and do what she could to help sell me the merchandise that I desperately wanted and that was just taking up space in the store; and, quite frankly, on the financial statement too.

Retailers continuously invest in training and educating their associates. But in so many cases it's not all about training but about hiring the "right" person to represent your brand. That sales associate should have personal characteristics and traits that reflect a service attitude. The fact is you can do all the training in the world and if the sales associates doesn't have a service "heart" and a genuine willingness to help the customer, it will leave a tremendous crack in your brand.

We all know that customer service is important; but, I would advocate that hiring a person that has a service attitude and reflects a willingness to help is just as important as investing in training. Both will reap the rewards of ultimately representing the best of your brand.

My Omnichannel Experiment

I never get to conduct experiments in my family. That is usually left up to our daughter. She loves anything science. We never know what we might find in a bowl or in the freezer. We call her the "mad scientist" and love (sort of) every gooey and smelly experiment that she conducts.

So, last week I decided to conduct my very own experiment based on a retail journey. It's not exactly scientific but let's call it my "Omnichannel" experience. I needed some materials and decided to order online and pick-up my purchase later at the store.

So, I set out to do my shopping one night while lounging and watching TV in the comfort of my home. Easy shopping, found it quickly, then searched for an online coupon code and found one, 40% off! I entered the promo code and I hit apply. Bingo, it worked! Off to a good start, my product is ordered and I got a discount. (But if I were in the store I would have definitely been able to use one competitor's coupon in addition to the store coupon). So, ordering online gave me convenience and my store discount, but because I didn't make my purchase in-store, I lost some savings by not being able to use a competitor's coupon, too.

The next step in my journey was that I received a

confirmation email from the store that they received my order. Also, my husband received a confirmation email (I added him as a second person that could pick up the purchase just in case I wouldn't be able to make time to get there).

Within one day after my initial communication I received notification that my purchase was ready for pick up. And, the notification listed the last possible day I could pick up my products.

A couple of days passed by and finally I set out one late morning to pick up my products that I ordered online. I parked in the store's lot, pushed the ignition button off and hit my timer on my smart phone. I thought, let me see how long this takes from parked car to pick up.

I entered the store and the first thing I saw was a stand-alone no-nonsense sign telling me exactly where to go to pick up my online order. **Signage was at the entrance!**

Image Credit: Jarvis Consultants, LLC

I went to the back of the store and there was a counter sign indicating "online pick-up". The associate asked my name, found my purchase, checked my license for ID all the while having a nice conversation. I got my purchase and stopped the timer. **Easy counter sign at pick-up location.**

Image Credit: Jarvis Consultants, LLC

From parked car to pick up it was a mere 4 minutes and 24 seconds. Wow! Under 5 minutes! That even takes into account that I stopped to read the sign, took photos of the sign up front and at the pick-up counter; and, I talked to the sales associate. You can't beat that if it's all about convenience and time.

I had my product in hand, so I didn't shop the store even though the retailer cleverly put the online pick up counter at the back of the store so I had to walk past merchandise.

The retailer is definitely driving traffic into the store with online pick up, but are they really driving more merchandise sales? I walked into the store, picked up my online purchase and walked out. So, based on my experiment, I would say no. But then again, I might not be the typical order online and pick up at store customer.

Just imagine if I picked up my order and the sales associate would have given me a reason to shop the store. What about here's a discount for shopping online only good to use in store right now? Very few can resist a deal! There's always something to purchase!

While my experiment didn't involve moths or shaving cream, it was still a fun journey for me and I plan on adding more Omnichannel experiences to my experiment list in the future.

By the way, in case you're wondering, the current experiment living in a bowl in my kitchen, is a moth and we're looking forward to seeing it become a beautiful butterfly!

Guess Where?

I know that this has been a realization for a while, and I have written about it before. But it still just amazes me that it's anybody's guess what store you might be in when you show merchandising photos. Recently we were looking for outdoor deck furniture. Nothing elaborate, because we have a limited amount of time to enjoy good weather here in the Northeast. Don't feel bad for us. There are some wonderful benefits to living on the East Coast, but unfortunately, weather isn't one of them.

We hit all of the usual retail suspects both brick and mortar (independents and mass) and online (specialty and mass).

So I thought it would be fun to play a guessing game with you. I included merchandising photos of five different stores (including grocery). Undoubtedly, some are obscure retailers (that we would never consider buying outdoor furniture from) to just make it that more interesting, I included them and, to make the point that every retailer is trying to sell seasonal merchandise.

Image Credit: Jarvis Consultants, LLC

Image Credit: Jarvis Consultants, LLC

Image Credit: Jarvis Consultants, LLC

Image Credit: Jarvis Consultants, LLC

Those of you who know the retail landscape probably got every guess correct. So, congratulations!

What was really interesting is that we ended up going to a retailer that has been in the news a lot lately (and not in a positive way).

Without fail, every brick and mortar sales associate (both mass and specialty) told us that there were more options online. We actually found a set we liked and we told the sales associate we would order it online. He immediately explained if we order it online without him that he doesn't get commission; so, we felt a little obligated to order with him. It wasn't the retailer's online store but its marketplace.

So, he sat down in front of the computer and we waded through pages and pages of outdoor furniture on their website and their marketplace. We decided on a set. The sales associate punched in my address, credit card, etc. It was more like a concierge service except we had to look at all of the photos with him as he worked the mouse scrolling through the options.

At the same time, we bought an umbrella and grill from the store to be delivered. Later, we found out that it was the sales associate's second day on the job, so we were especially glad that we took the extra time and made the sale with him.

And in case you're still guessing the retailer locations of the above photos, I have to tell you I took these photos over the course of early to late spring; so, it's anybody's guess.

Is Shopping Giving You Blurry Vision?

As mentioned, I live in the Northeast. So, my daughter just went back to school last week. My nieces and nephews who live in other parts of the country have been back to school for nearly a month or more.

I have worked in the b-to-b retail industry for most of my career. I am well aware of the continued consolidation, channels blurring with retailers trying to capture the total market basket with product categories being sold across retail lines. But, shopping for back-to-school supplies made my vision blurry!

This year in particular, I didn't know which store I was shopping. I could have been anywhere. Regardless of the retailer's core category, the back to school seasonal products are in heavy pursuit from every type of retailer. I literally saw back-to-school promotions and products in grocery chains, dollar stores, office supplies, discounters, mass merchants, drug chains and need I go on? From the traditional mass discounters like Walmart and Target to specialty stores like Bed Bath & Beyond and Staples to chain-stores like CVS and Stop and Shop; and, let's not even touch the options to buy school supplies online.

So many convenient choices for the consumer that helps to meet the needs of busy shoppers. Need milk and bread from a grocer? You are there so you might as well pick up the needed school supplies. Need computer ink from an office supply store? Might as well grab the school supplies. And why not, retailers are always looking for seasonal categories that can contribute to their gross profit margins.

Retail Dive reports that parents are expected to shell out an average $1,642 on student expenses this year, up 33% from 2015's average of $1,239, according to the latest American Express Spending & Saving Tracker.

As stores continue to chase product categories that add to the convenience of its shoppers (and to its bottom line) they start to blur. Please leave all of your preconceived notions at the "entrance" and just shop for what you need versus shopping for what you think the store carries. You'll be so surprised at check out how many of your product needs were met. Your vision might get a little blurry; and, upon "exiting" the store you just might have to glance back to confirm exactly where you were shopping.

When Will I See You Again?

Beginning with Black Friday and running until days after Christmas are considered the most anticipated and expected shopping days of the year. These holiday months of shopping make a difference in whether it is a good or bad year for most retailers' financial statements. Because, once the holiday season is over retailers know how hard it is to even maintain a fraction of the shopping frenzy experienced during that time period.

When post-holiday season kicks-in, consumers get back to life, frugality, diets, disciplines - you name it -- whatever New Year's resolution promise we made.

During this down period, retailers turn their focus to getting us back in the stores. Sometimes that focus can make our shopping experience a little confusing.

Here is my recent confusing shopping experience. My daughter needed a Valentine's Day craft classroom project, so I had to go shopping. (Of course I did research first online).

Stepping in the stores, I was immediately hit with Valentine's Day and Easter all at once. It was overwhelming with holiday merchandise competing against one another. Plus, I thought, "Really? Easter already? Ash

Wednesday hasn't even happened!".

Confusing because retailers are not sure when they will see us again; so they merchandise every possible holiday in hopes of enticing us to purchase something - anything.

While retailers see it as creating excitement in the stores, it can sometimes appear to shoppers as if retailers are grasping for dollars, and to me, it's a turn off.

But after I was done shopping (I hit three different stores), I thought about my afternoon smiling and embracing the journey; because, ultimately, all of the different holiday merchandise was their way of welcoming me back into the stores by making sure that they had something that I liked.

They were waiting for my return, and happy to see me again!

Will You Remember This Time As "Back In The Day"?

Back in the day, you had to plan your shopping trips from groceries to furniture.

Now, online retail has changed the way we approach shopping. There is an engaged escalation of buying all kinds of products (and services for that matter) online. Consumers are getting comfortable with making daily purchases online. Even the rare person that does not buy online surely has someone in their life that brags about how easy and convenient it is to purchase online. A Pew research 2016 report shows that eight in 10 Americans are now shopping online. I am guessing that by now, that is obviously an even bigger number.

Our mobile devices allow us to purchase all sorts of things on the go. I just saw a commercial where it happened in the middle of the desert (and was delivered the same day). What about the ability to quickly and accurately do a competitive price check without getting in-and-out of our cars? Purchases can also happen from the comfort of our own home or office. Definitely different than my Mother's shopping trips back in the day.

While all of this is true, online retail sales still only represents a small portion of total retail sales. The U.S. Commerce Department reported that consumers spent nearly $350 billion online in 2016; that's up double digits from the previous year but only 12% of total sales.

I believe that online shopping is elevating the consumers experience in-store because brick and mortar retailers know that they have to compete. They compete on merchandising, on customer service and you can name whatever physical in-store shopping benefit is important to you. It's new to them but they are fighting to understand it, figure it out and gain more customers for their stores through the online retail marketplace. Each shopping experience educates the shopper and makes us better customers for all types of retailers. How retailers embrace our shopping behavior and leverage our preferences to create loyalty is up to them.

Please do not get me wrong. I am not pushing online shopping. I am merely stating the obvious, that shoppers are benefiting from the evolution of retail. And, most shoppers, like myself, find it liberating to have choices. For example, I love shopping stores and experiencing the merchandising, lay-out and customer service. Sometimes I just need to see it, touch it and talk face-to-face with a floor salesperson. Other times, I like shopping online. Whether it is an easy buy and I need it in a hurry; or I do not have the time or energy to run from store-to-store. So, I order it online. (I confess I have ordered a couch or two online). It is nice to have options.

So, I wonder how my daughter's era (who are referred to as digital natives) will look back to our days and refer to our retail shopping experiences? This is surely just the beginning of the evolution of retail. I am sure I will fondly remember this time and refer to it as "back in the day".

"Whatever you are, be a good one."

Abraham Lincoln

Conclusion

It's always easier to recognize a learning moment once we have walked through the encounter; but, there are those rare moments when we recognize a lesson learned, when it is actually happening. In most cases, we tend to learn "after the fact".

The hope of this book, adapted from Sonya's Blog, captures learning moments from everyday encounters through the eyes of an MBA marketer, Entrepreneur, SBO, wife and Mom. Chronicling the journey with like themes and putting the lessons in context, allows all of us to see common themes and occurrences which enables us to rise, and, learn from them.

These themes are prevalent and obvious in most of our lives on a daily basis. If we journey with our eyes wide open, each and every day, creating our contributions to live through passion and/or causes and allows us to live out our dreams.

Understanding these learning moments helps us to experience life to its fullest - both business and personal. We need to stretch ourselves and use each teaching moment to successfully execute.

Creating, Learning, Executing and Experiencing helps us to better understand life. Like I said in the beginning, life is short. This is not a dress rehearsal. It is the real thing!

I will continue to find mindful minutes in my everyday experiences through my eyes as a Marketer. My hope is that this book was able to share a glimpse of the important lessons I learned, use them as teaching moments, and for all of us to ultimately learn from them and to keep moving forward.

Sonya Ruff Jarvis

Thank you for experiencing *Mindful Minutes: A Marketer's Journey Through Business.*

Please provide your review at Amazon.com.

COMING SOON:

Mindful Minutes: A Marketer's Journey Through Branding and *Mindful Minutes: A Marketer's Journey Through Event Marketing* by Sonya Ruff Jarvis.

About The Author

Sonya Ruff Jarvis is the Managing Member of Jarvis Consultants and Founder of the eRetailer Summit and JC Event Group. Sonya has extensive experience in creating original, innovative solutions to overcome major business challenges. As the Managing Member of Jarvis Consultants, Sonya brings 20+ years of business experience, having previously served in executive roles responsible for designing, launching and managing complex projects across diverse global industries. For more information, please go to www.linkedin.com/in/jarvisconsultants.

Jarvis Consultants provides customized consulting services in strategic development, marketing & promotion and event management. Services span across a broad array of industries with core expertise in DIY hardware/home improvement, retail, distribution channels, gaming and publishing/media. For more information, please go to www.jarvisconsultants.com.

The Home Improvement eRetailer Summit is an annual face-to-face event that connects the entire retail ecommerce home improvement marketplace. It brings the right channel partners together to network, gain intelligence and insights about home improvement ecommerce. The Summit offers curated educational sessions, crafted by an advisory council of influencers. For more information, please go to www.eretailersummit.com.

Sonya earned her M.B.A. in Marketing from New York Institute of Technology and a Bachelor of Arts degree with a major in Communications and minor in Sociology from Hiram College. Sonya is married and she and her husband have a daughter residing in Fairfield County Connecticut.

You can follow Sonya on Twitter at @jarvisconsult and @eretailersummit.

Mindful Minutes
A Marketer's Journey Through Business

By
Sonya Ruff Jarvis

Sonya Ruff Jarvis writes a captivating book using everyday experiences, identified and used as "Mindful Minutes" to help you leverage common mistakes and accomplishments made by others while building a successful business.

Mindful Minutes: A Marketer's Journey Through Business, captures learning moments from everyday encounters through the eyes of an MBA marketer, Entrepreneur, SBO, wife and mom. Sonya chronicles the journey with like themes, while putting the lessons in context to allow the reader to see the commonalities and occurrences; ultimately allowing you to learn from them. This book is based o Sonya's Blog: Breaking the Code of Excellence, a Jarvis Consultants LLC product.

This is the first of a series of "Mindful Minutes" books with similar themes. Start collecting yours now with this one - "A Marketer's Journey Through Business" and look for future *Mindful Minutes*: "A Marketer's Journey Through Branding" and "A Marketer's Journey Through Event Marketing".

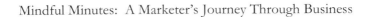

28 And we know that in all things God works for the good of those who love him, who have been called according to his purpose.

Romans 8:28 NIV

Sonya Ruff Jarvis

Enhanced DNA Publishing
www.EnhancedDNAPublishing.com

Made in the USA
Columbia, SC
30 April 2019